Dropping In On...

INDIA

Lewis K. Parker

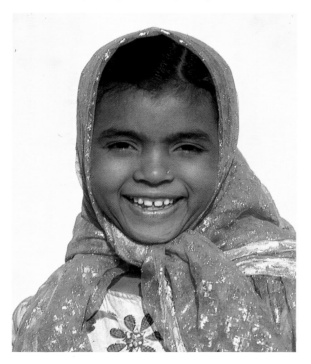

A Geography Series

ROURKE BOOK COMPANY, INC.
VERO BEACH, FLORIDA 32964

A Blackbirch Graphics book.

Printed in the United States of America.

Library of Congress Cataloging-in-Publication Data

Parker, Lewis K.
    India / Lewis K. Parker.
       p.   cm. — (Dropping in on)
    Includes index.
    ISBN 1-55916-005-5
    1. India—Description and travel—
Juvenile literature. I. Title. II. Series.
    DS414.2.P37   1994
    915.4—dc20   94-614
                                          CIP
                                          AC

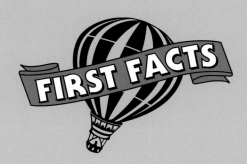

India
....

Official Name: **Republic of India**

Area: **1,266,600 square miles**

Population: **897,400,000**

Capital: **New Delhi**

Largest City: **Greater Bombay**

Highest Elevation:
K2 (28,250 feet)

Official Language: **Hindi (English is the "associate official" language)**

Major Religions: **Hindu, Islam**

Money: **Rupee**

Form of Government:
Federal republic

TABLE OF CONTENTS

Our Blue Ball—The Earth

The Earth can be divided into two hemispheres. The word hemisphere means "half a ball"—in this case, the ball is the Earth.

The equator is an imaginary line that runs around the middle of the Earth. It separates the Northern Hemisphere from the Southern Hemisphere. North America—where Canada, the United States, and Mexico are located—is in the Northern Hemisphere.

The Northern Hemisphere

When the North Pole is tilted toward the sun, the sun's most powerful rays strike the northern half of the Earth and less sunshine hits the Southern Hemisphere. That is when people in the Northern Hemisphere enjoy summer. When

the North Pole is tilted away from the sun, and the Southern Hemisphere receives the most sunshine, the seasons reverse. Then winter comes to the Northern Hemisphere. Seasons in the Northern Hemisphere and the Southern Hemisphere are always opposite.

Get Ready for India

Hop into your hot-air balloon. Let's take a trip! You are about to drop in on India, a country in Asia. India is in the Northern Hemisphere. It is about one third the size of the United States, but it has a larger population. More than 890 million people live here. That is almost 3 times the population of the United States.

India is shaped like a triangle. The far northern area has high, rugged mountains. These are the Himalayas, which are some of the highest mountains in the world. Below the mountains lie fertile plains. The Ganges River flows through these plains. Some of this area is gently rolling land with dark, rich soil that is good for farming. Most of the people of India live in this area.

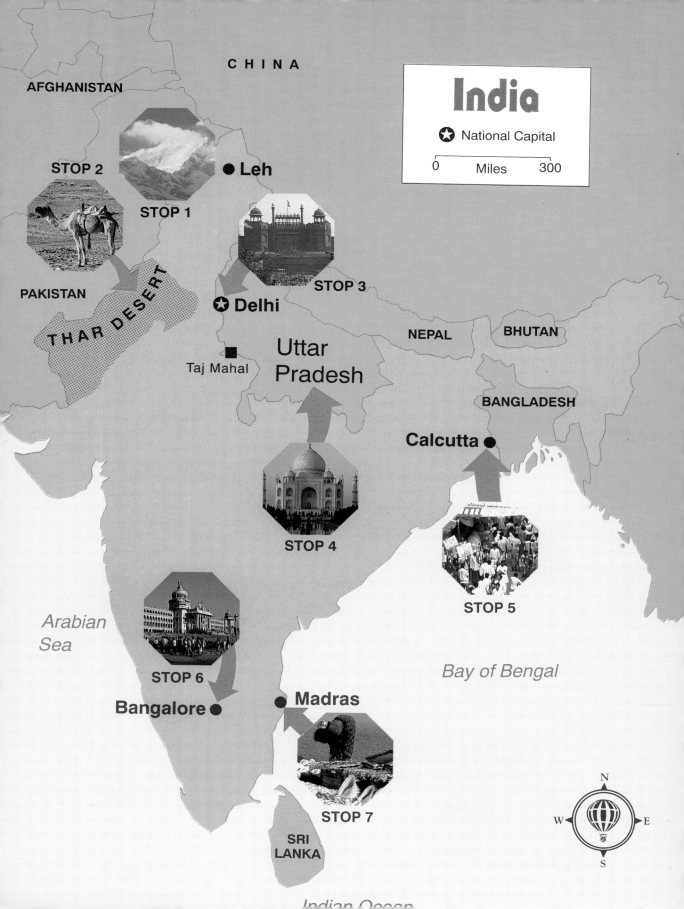

CHINA

AFGHANISTAN

India

⭐ National Capital

0   Miles   300

STOP 2

● Leh

STOP 1

STOP 3

PAKISTAN

THAR DESERT

✪ **Delhi**

NEPAL

BHUTAN

Taj Mahal

Uttar
Pradesh

BANGLADESH

Calcutta ●

STOP 4

STOP 5

*Arabian
Sea*

STOP 6

Bay of Bengal

Bangalore ●

● **Madras**

STOP 7

SRI
LANKA

N
W   E
S

Indian Ocean

Opposite: Clouds brush the peaks of Mount Kanchenjunga, high in the Himalayas.

Stop 1: Leh

Our first stop will be in northern India near the border of China, high in the Himalayas. The snow never melts on the peaks of the Himalayas. In fact, the name "Himalaya" means "home of snow." Trains cannot cross the Himalayas, but you can take a road up into the mountains.

The town of Leh is in a fertile valley between the peaks of the mountains. Leh is a quiet town, where the mountain people greet you with *julle* (pronounced jew-lay). *Julle* means both "hello" and "good-bye." High in the mountains the air is thin and dry, and not easy to breathe.

You can see many mountain goats and black bears in the Himalayas. Yaks also wander through the pasture lands. Shepherds travel across the mountains in search of valleys, where there will be grass for their herds of goats.

A woman from the Ladakh region of India.

Leh ①

Arabian
Sea

Bay of Bengal

N
W — E
S

Indian Ocean

Desert.

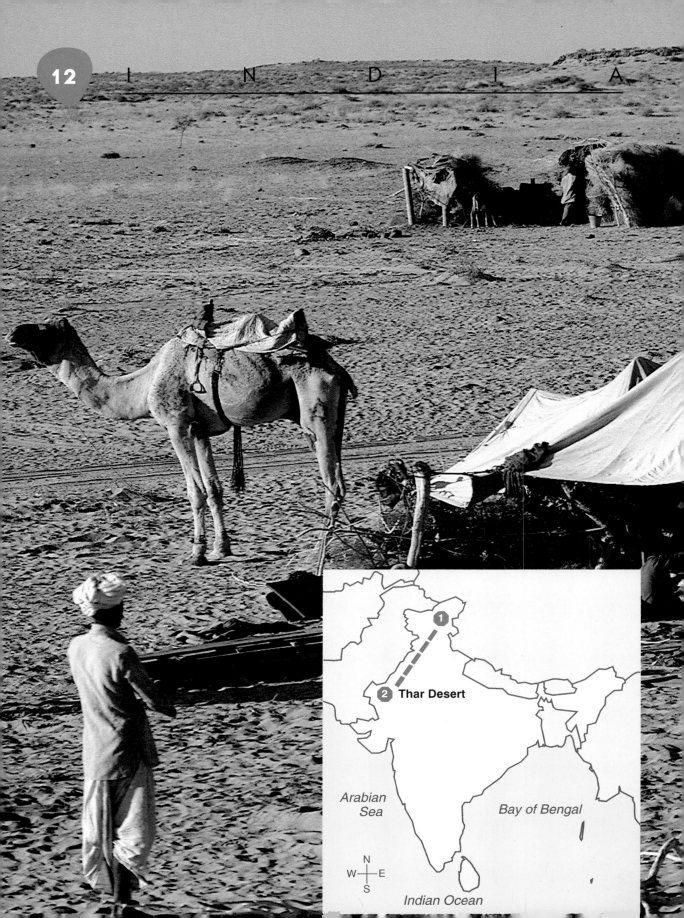

Thar Desert

Arabian Sea

Bay of Bengal

N
W E
S

Indian Ocean

Stop 2: Thar Desert

    The Thar Desert is a bleak place in India's northwestern corner. It is a large, sandy wasteland that stretches 300 miles wide and 500 miles long—an area larger than the state of California! This desert crosses from India into Pakistan, and is one of the driest areas on Earth. It receives only about 10 inches of rain each year.

Travelers rest at a camel drivers' station in the Thar Desert.

Growing Up in India

An Indian boy grins at the camera.

About 80 percent of all Indian people live in villages. If you lived in an Indian village, you might live in a mud hut that has 3 rooms. One room is the kitchen, and 2 rooms are used for sleeping. You would take off your shoes before entering the house, and sit on a mat on the floor.

Boys and girls wear different kinds of clothing. Most girls and women wear *saris*. A *sari* is a dress made of a long piece of cotton or silk cloth. The cloth may be 25 feet in length. The cloth is wound gracefully around the body and draped over the head to form a hood. Boys and men often wear a *dhoti*. This is a piece of white cloth wound around the waist. *Dhotis* look like comfortable, baggy pants. Most men wear turbans. Everyone may wear sandals, go barefoot, or wear shoes.

Now, we'll leave the desert to travel directly **east** *to Delhi.*

A young Indian girl holds her puppy.

Stop 3: Delhi

Delhi is a crowded city of more than 8 million people. The first thing you might notice about Delhi is that it is made of two large towns, called Old Delhi and New Delhi.

Old Delhi has a bazaar, or marketplace, along Chandni Chauk, which is the widest street in Old Delhi. The streets of the bazaar are narrow and lined with dozens of small shops and open air markets. You can find all kinds of things here such as jewelry, brass pots, rugs, paintings, perfumes, and incense sticks. Some shops sell expensive gems, such as rubies.

New Delhi has many parks, fountains, and wide avenues. These avenues come together in places called circles. These are broad, circular areas. Some of the government buildings are located here.

A large crowd shops at the busy bazaar along the Chandni Chauk.

Animals in India

A monkey sits among some leaves in a tree.

More than 500 species of mammals exist in India. You can see many mountain goats in the Himalayas, panthers in the southern forests, and tigers and lions in a small area of the northwest plains. Many kinds of deer and antelope live in protected areas throughout India, such as the Indian gazelle, Indian antelope, *nilgai* "blue bull," swamp deer, spotted deer, barking deer, and tiny mouse deer. Rhinos also live in protected areas. In forests, and on the plains, you can see wild water buffalo, wild pigs, foxes, sloth bears, striped hyenas, and wild dogs called *dhole*.

An elephant helps its master move a large tree trunk.

A white tiger stops to take a drink of water.

More than 2,000 kinds of birds live in India. The list includes hornbills, eagles, owls, pelicans, cranes, storks, and ibises.

Monkeys are the most commonly seen animals in India. The sacred langur is seen everywhere, especially in temples.

Elephants are especially important to Indian people. They are trained to lift and move heavy objects with their trunks. Elephants help people clear forests and build homes.

*For our next stop, we'll journey **southeast** to Uttar Pradesh.*

Stop 4: Uttar Pradesh

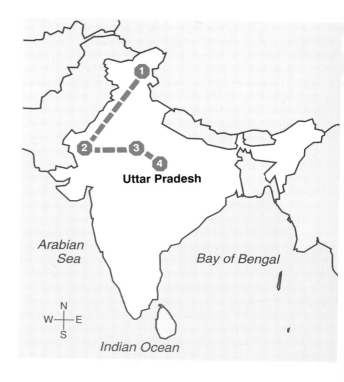

Uttar Pradesh is one of the largest states in India. It has more people than any other Indian state. About 140 million people live here. Uttar Pradesh is known as a great religious center because the holy Ganges River flows through it. Thousands of Hindus come to Uttar Pradesh to worship at this river.

The city of Agra is in west central Uttar Pradesh, along the Yamuna River.

The Taj Mahal is located here beside the Yamuna River. This is one of the most beautiful buildings in the world. The Taj Mahal is a huge tomb, or burial place, that Shah Jahan built for his beloved wife. In the 1630s, more than 20,000 people worked to construct the building.

Opposite: The Taj Mahal is reflected in a pool. Sheets of white marble decorated with gems were used to cover this building.

The Ganges River

The Ganges River begins very high in the Himalayas. It flows out of an ice cave 13,800 feet high in the mountains. On its journey through India, the Ganges is fed by many smaller rivers. It travels 1,560 miles to the Bay of Bengal. To millions of Hindu people, the Ganges is sacred. They call it *Gangama*—Mother Ganges.

Hindus come from all over India to the Ganges. For Hindus, the trip is a religious journey. They hope that when they die, they will be near the Ganges. Then their bodies will be cremated, or burned, and the ashes thrown into the holy water.

Hindus drink the water of the Ganges. They believe that the river is a living thing.

*Our next stop will be Calcutta. To get there, we'll travel a long way **southeast** to the Bay of Bengal.*

In the holy city of Benares, Hindus bathe in the Ganges.

A busy market in Calcutta.

Stop 5: Calcutta

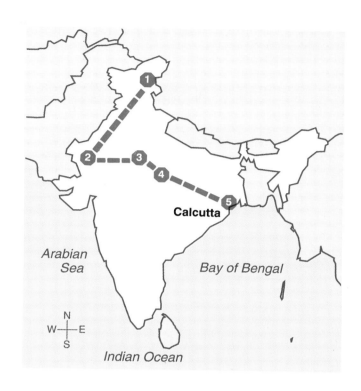

Calcutta is located near the Hooghly River on a plain that extends into the Bay of Bengal. It is the second-largest city in India. More than 10 million people live here. India's chief port for trade with southeast Asia, Calcutta is a busy trading center. Hundreds of thousands of people work in mills that process jute, which is a plant

fiber. These factories turn jute into burlap bags. Other factories make metal goods, paint, and shoes.

Calcutta is a hot, crowded city. As you travel its streets, you will see pedicabs (small carriages pulled by people on bicycles), cows, beggars sleeping in alleys, and huge groups of people.

A pedicab.

Let's now leave Calcutta and head **southwest** *to Bangalore.*

Stop 6: Bangalore

Bangalore is a large city in the plateau region of southern India. Almost 5 million people live here. Bangalore is a modern city with many schools and colleges. It is known for its big aircraft factory and for other products, such as carpets, tobacco, silk, cotton, and silver.

As you stroll through Bangalore, you'll notice many parks, gardens, and wide avenues lined with trees. It also has tall office buildings and open-air markets. Many people come here to find work, start businesses, or get an education.

Just inside the city are the Kolar Gold Fields. You can visit this major gold producing area, which may have the deepest pits in the world. You can go down into shafts that are more than 1 mile deep.

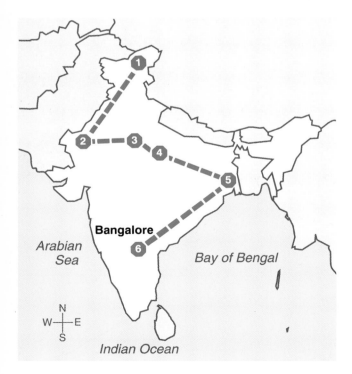

🎈 *For our last stop, we will travel directly **east** to Madras.*

Beautiful buildings line the streets of Bangalore.

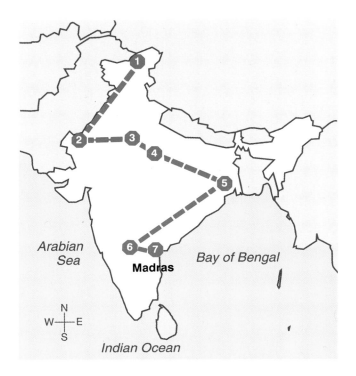

Stop 7: Madras

Madras is on the southeast coast of India. The city has a tropical climate, and it is always very hot and humid here. Many people who live in and around Madras speak Tamil. This is the oldest language in the world. However, English is also spoken in Madras. Because of its location on the Bay of Bengal, Madras is a major shipping center. Its harbor is always busy with ships that are coming and going.

When you want to get away from the heat of the city, you can stretch out on the beach just outside Madras. The beach borders the Bay of Bengal and cool breezes blow in from the bay.

Vendors display different kinds of seashells for sale at Marina Beach.

Now it's time to set sail for home. When you return, you can think back on the wonderful adventure you had in India.

Indian Words in the English Language

The English language has borrowed several words that were first used in India. Here are just a few of these words.

bungalow A one-story house with a veranda, first built in India; the word comes from the Hindi language and means "belonging to Bengal."

cashmere Very fine wool of a mountain goat from Kashmir, an area in India.

dungarees Jeans; the word comes from the Hindi word *dugri* and is the coarse fabric worn by poorer Indians.

pajama A garment for sleeping or casual wear, consisting of a top and comfortable pants.

punch A mixture of alcohol, water, sugar, lemon, and spice; from the Hindi word *panch*.

shampoo From the Hindi word *champo*, which means "press."

thug A member of a band of robbers and murderers; from the Hindi word *thag*.

Further Reading

Cumming, David. *India*. New York: Franklin Watts, 1991.

Ganeri, Anita. *Journey Through India*. Mahwah, NJ: Troll, 1993.

Haskins, Jim. *Count Your Way Through India*. Minneapolis, MN: Carolrhoda Books, 1990.

Kalman, Bobbie. *India: The Culture*. New York: Crabtree Publications, 1990.

_____. *India: The People*. New York: Crabtree Publications, 1990.

Kaur, Sharon. *Food in India*. Vero Beach, FL: Rourke, 1989.

Schmidt, Jeremy. *In the Village of the Elephants*. New York: Walker, 1994.

Singh, Anne. *Living in India*. Ossining, NY: Young Discovery, 1988.

Index

Acknowledgments and Photo Credits
Cover and pages 10, 11, 14, 15, 18, 19, 20, 24, 25, 27, 29:
Air-India Library; pp. 4, 6: National Aeronautics and Space
Administration; pp. 12, 16: ©Porterfield/Chickering/Photo
Researchers, Inc.; p. 23: ©Walter S. Clark/Photo Researchers, Inc.
Maps by Blackbirch Graphics, Inc.

DEMCO